Homosexuality

Homosexuality

Robert E. Dunbar

—Issues in Focus—

ENSLOW PUBLISHERS, INC.

44 Fadem Road	P.O. Box 38
Box 699	Aldershot
Springfield, N.J. 07081	Hants GU12 6BP
U.S.A.	U.K.

Library of Congress Cataloging-in-Publication Data

Dunbar, Robert E.
     Homosexuality / Robert E. Dunbar.
        p. cm. — (Issues in focus)
     Includes bibliographical references (p.) and index.
     ISBN 0-89490-665-8
       1. Homosexuality—United States—Juvenile literature. 2. Gay
rights—United States—Juvenile literature. I. Title.
II. Series: Issues in focus (Springfield, N.J.)
HQ76.26.D85 1995
306.76'6—dc20
                                   95-18088
                                      CIP
                                      AC

Printed in the United States of America

10 9 8 7 6 5 4 3 2 1

Illustration Credits: AP/Wide World Photos, pp. 30, 52, 58, 79, 83, 86,
92; *The Bangor Daily News*, pp. 35, 54, 65, 70, 73; *Christianity Today*, p.
49; HarperCollins, p. 21; Reprinted by permission of the Kinsey Institute
for Research in Sex, Gender, and Reproduction, Inc., photograph by
Dellenback, p. 16; St. Martin's Press, photo by James D. Wilson, p. 41;
The Unitarian Church, Bangor, Maine, p. 62; White House, pp. 9, 37.

Cover Illustration: AP/Wide World Photos.

Contents

1

Society and Homosexual Orientation

The great majority of humans are heterosexually oriented, that is, males and females are sexually attracted to each other. But when someone is homosexually oriented, this means that he or she is sexually attracted to persons of the same gender. Males who are attracted to males are known as "gays." Females attracted sexually to females are referred to as "lesbians." Both are often identified collectively as "gays." Those who are sexually attracted to both males and females are called "bisexuals."

For generations, homosexual orientation was whispered about, feared as an aberration—the ultimate sexual shame. Anyone in the least suspected of having this sexual orientation was often firmly shunned. Any evidence of homosexual practice carried with it the threat of legal prosecution, heavy fines, and imprisonment.

And yet, homosexual orientation has always been an element, albeit usually a minor one, of every culture and society known to humans. In many cultures it has often been little understood, rarely accepted or tolerated by the majority, often savagely opposed and rejected on religious grounds, especially in cultures dominated by Christians, Moslems, and Jews.

Yet it has never been eradicated, no matter how forceful or powerful the social pressures or legal restrictions have been. Homosexual orientation, advocates argue, is a fact of life that should be fully accepted by all members of society. That and other arguments in defense of homosexual orientation have gained more and more public attention over the past three decades.

The Sexual Revolution

The impetus for this change in public attitude in America came with the sexual revolution of the late 1960s and with it the Gay Liberation Movement. The wellspring for that movement was the Stonewall Riot in New York's Greenwich Village in 1969.[1] With this demonstration, gays and lesbians sent a message that they were no longer willing to accept what they believed to be unfair and illegal harassment by the police and other authorities. From that point on, politically active gays grew in number and political power. They became organized enough to claim a politically significant block of more than two million voters, large enough to attract the attention of presidential candidates.

One of them, Bill Clinton, had listened sympathetically to demands for gay rights and promised to do something about it if he was elected. As president,

When President Bill Clinton met with leaders of the gay rights movement on April 16, 1993, it was the first time such a meeting had taken place in the White House.

he attempted to make good on his campaign promise by lifting the ban on gays serving in the military, but this stirred up a violent storm of controversy. This ended, at least temporarily, in a compromise that was unsatisfactory to both sides, the gays and the antigays. This will be discussed more fully in a later chapter.

Among the antigays who are most opposed to acceptance of homosexual orientation and lifestyle are members of the Southern Baptist Convention (SBC). In 1992, the SBC amended its constitution to bar any SBC church that acts "to affirm, approve, or endorse homosexual behavior."[2] Many other church organizations in all sections of the country were divided on how to address or deal with the challenge of openly accepting gays in the military. They were also divided on how to respond to other challenges posed by advocates of gay rights. As the power of gay advocacy groups grew, however, the moral attitude of these and other groups opposed to homosexual orientation hardened.

Not An Illness

For a long time, homosexual orientation had been classified as an illness, evidence of sexual dysfunction and other psychological abnormalities. But this definition was dropped in 1973 when the American Psychiatric Association (an organization composed of practicing psychiatrists) removed homosexuality from its official list of mental disorders. Two years later, in 1975, the American Psychological Association (a group of psychology teachers, researchers, and practicing psychologists) adopted the following resolution:

> Homosexuality, per se, implies no impairment in judgment, stability, reliability, or general social or

10

vocational capabilities. Further, the American Psychological Association urges all mental health professionals to take the lead in removing the stigma of mental illness that has long been associated with homosexual orientations.[3]

Several years after that resolution was made public, the American Psychological Association established the Task Force on Lesbian and Gay Concerns. In 1991, the Task Force declared that for more than twenty years the APA had encouraged psychiatrists, psychotherapists, and other mental health practitioners to accept homosexuality as a bona fide sexual orientation "and to provide unbiased and appropriate services to lesbians and gay men. The 1990s should be a time for renewed commitment to this important principle."[4]

What Makes Someone Gay

Declaring that homosexual orientation was not an illness, however, did nothing to explain to the general public what causes it. Nor could science satisfactorily explain to parents why a child of theirs was gay or lesbian. One organization, founded in 1973, the same year the APA declared that homosexual orientation was not an illness, has attempted to answer the question by surveying scientists who have studied various aspects of sexual orientation. The name of the organization is Parents and Friends of Lesbians and Gays, Inc. (PFLAG).

According to PFLAG's survey, the exact causes of heterosexuality and homosexuality are unknown. However, a predisposition toward a homosexual, bisexual, or heterosexual orientation is present at birth in all boys and girls. Whatever a child's sexual orientation happens

11

to be, it is likely to be the result of the interaction of several different factors, including genetics, hormones, and the environment.[5]

Many studies have been made of relationships between parents and their children in attempts to identify the causes of homosexuality. For instance, if a boy has an unusually close relationship with his mother and is neglected by his father, this may result in a total rejection of members of the opposite sex as sexual partners. However, scientific studies have shown that this is *not the cause* of homosexuality.

The Conservative Religious Point of View

Any scientific explanation of the causes of homosexual orientation, however, is unlikely to satisfy those who are fundamentally opposed to it on a religious and/or moral basis. Religious fundamentalists in particular claim that there is ample testimony in the Old Testament of the Bible that God has condemned any form of homosexual orientation. This is a sin that no honest Christian can tolerate. They might love the sinner as evidence of their Christian compassion, but they can never love or accept the sin.

Both Sides of the Controversy

In the chapters that follow you will be reading about both sides of this controversy. You will discover what people think and say publicly and privately about homosexual orientation and why it has been so difficult to talk about it openly. You will read how people reacted to the murder of a gay young man in Maine and how the case was resolved.

Important scientific developments in the study of what causes sexual orientation will be reviewed, and so will the aftereffects of the Gay Revolution and its impact on laws affecting the rights of the homosexually oriented.

By the time you finish reading and studying this book you will have a better understanding of the conflicting viewpoints on the subject of homosexuality.

2

What Science Can Tell Us

Public discussion of homosexual orientation did not begin to surface until sex researcher Alfred C. Kinsey published his startling revelations in 1948 in a book titled *Sexual Behavior in the Human Male.*[1] In this study of 5,300 male volunteers, Kinsey and his associates reported that about 50 percent or one half of those surveyed had had a same-sex (homosexual) genital experience before puberty. The onset of puberty usually begins at age twelve or thirteen in males, age ten or eleven in females.

This was surprising news, especially to those who believed that the great majority of men and women were born with an exclusively heterosexual orientation. They were even more surprised to learn that, according to the Kinsey study, a full 25 percent—one in four of those interviewed—said they had had more than incidental

15

Alfred C. Kinsey (left) speaking with a colleague at his institute of sex research.

homosexual experience for at least three years between the ages of sixteen and fifty-five. An even larger percentage—37 percent—had had at least one homosexual experience leading to orgasm after puberty. The smallest group—10 percent—said they had been exclusively homosexual for a period of at least three years between the ages of sixteen and fifty-five.

Five years later, in 1953, Kinsey and his associates published the results of studies with females, *Sexual Behavior in the Human Female*. These results were also surprising, but they showed much less involvement in homosexual activity among women. Only 13 percent had had a homosexual experience to orgasm prior to age forty-five. Only 2 to 3 percent reported having exclusively homosexual experience.

A More Liberal Attitude

The sexual revolution of the late 1960s and early 1970s brought a more liberal attitude toward human sexuality. This liberality carried over into the feminist movement, which brought women more freedom of self-expression, including sexual expression. In spite of these developments, the Kinsey figures for homosexual activity remained fairly constant up until the early 1990s, when a new study was conducted by the National Opinion Research Center at the University of Chicago.

Interviews for the study were conducted in person by 220 researchers over a period of several months in 1992. About four out of five people contacted agreed to be surveyed. In addition to responding to the questions asked by the researchers in person, those interviewed were given written forms to complete and place in sealed envelopes. In this way, the answers they had given orally could be checked against what they wrote privately about some of the more potentially embarrassing questions.

The results of this study were first made public in October 1994. It was based on surveys of 3,432 men and women eighteen to fifty-nine years of age. Some sex researchers considered it more important than the studies by Kinsey and others who relied on interviews with volunteers, who tend to be more interested in sex and more sexually active. However, in this study, as in the Kinsey studies and those that followed, all of those interviewed had to give their consent.

When the results of the study were made public, it was also announced that two versions would be published: a paperback version by the University of Chicago Press, titled *The Social Organization of Sexuality*, by John H. Gagnon, Edward O. Laumann, Robert T. Michael, and Stuart Michaels; and, in hardcover, *Sex in America: A Definitive Survey*, by Gagnon, Laumann, Michael, and *The New York Times* science reporter Gina Kolata, to be published by Little, Brown and Company.

The new study reported that only 2.8 percent of the men and 1.4 percent of the women interviewed identified themselves as homosexual or bisexual. The incidence of homosexual experience was higher, with 9 percent of the men and 5 percent of the women having had at least one homosexual experience since puberty. Almost half of those men, 40 percent of the 9 percent, had had the experience before they were eighteen but had not had one since. Most of the women were eighteen or older before they had their first homosexual experience.

Those surveyed were also asked if having sex with someone of the same gender was appealing. The idea was somewhat or very appealing to 5.5 percent of the women, while 6 percent of the men said they were attracted to other men.

Born That Way?

As yet, there has been no conclusive proof that the only reason a person is homosexually oriented is that he or she was born that way. Nor is it an accepted fact that a person's sexual orientation is entirely due to experiences and behavior learned in childhood and adolescence. However, recent evidence has shown that every human being is born with a sexual potential or preference for either heterosexual, homosexual, or bisexual orientation.[2] It is also an accepted fact that a person may be born with no sexual orientation or preference. In this case, the person's sexual orientation is *asexual.*

Whatever potential a person happens to be born with, the preference for a specific orientation will be felt and enhanced by experiences during childhood and adolescence. Before becoming an adult, a person will know what his or her sexual orientation is. For example, Dr. John Money, a professor of medical psychology at Johns Hopkins University in Baltimore, believes that the ages of five through eight are particularly important in establishing whether a person's erotic attraction will be toward someone of the opposite or the same sex. He declared, "Homosexuality as well as heterosexuality is ultimately defined by the sex of the partner with whom one is capable of falling in love."

Studies have shown that many gay and lesbian young

people had childhood crushes on other children and adults of their own gender. There were frequently other indicators of sexual orientation as well. One young man recalled, "I always knew that I was gay. When I was eight or nine I would steal my mother's *Playgirl* magazines and look at the pictures of men. I also remember seeing heterosexual couples and knowing I wasn't like that."

In explaining why he had decided to "come out of the closet" and tell his family and friends he was gay, another young man recalled what made him realize that his sexual orientation was homosexual.

> The realization for me came when I knew that I wasn't attracted to women in a sexual way. After trying a heterosexual relationship with a girl, I knew that I was not meeting my emotional needs by being with her. I needed to feel love from a man, not from a woman.

Although the idea that homosexual orientation is a disease has been rejected by the leading psychological and medical associations, homosexuality remains a controversial issue. Those homosexuals who are depressed or unhappy about their orientation and want to change it to heterosexual can still seek psychiatric help and counseling and choose to undergo conversion therapy.

Even with a strong desire and determination, however, success is not guaranteed. In a study by sex researchers Masters and Johnson, fifty-four males and thirteen females requested therapy to change their sexual orientation from homosexual to heterosexual.[3] Yet a follow-up study five years later showed that there was a failure rate of 28 percent. Some critics of the study have

Sex researchers William H. Masters, M.D., and Virginia E. Johnson contributed to the new openness about sexual matters that characterized the sexual revolution.

argued that those who were able to change their sexual orientation may have had the ability to do so without having to undergo conversion therapy. In 1990, the American Psychological Association declared that:

> Scientific evidence does not show that conversion therapy works and that it can do more harm than good. Changing one's sexual orientation is not simply a matter of changing one's sexual behavior. It would require altering one's emotional, romantic, and sexual feelings and restructuring one's self-concept and social identity.
>
> Although some mental health providers do attempt sexual orientation conversion, others question the ethics of trying to alter through therapy a trait that is not a disorder and that is extremely important to an individual's identity. Not all gays and lesbians who seek therapy want to change their sexual orientation. Gays and lesbians may seek counseling for any of the same reasons as anyone else. In addition, they may seek psychological help to "come out" or to deal with prejudice, discrimination, and violence.

Answering the Mental Illness Question

The question of whether homosexual orientation is a mental illness was first studied in the late 1950s by Dr. Evelyn Hooker of the University of California at Los Angeles. She found no differences in emotional stability and mental health between men who were homosexually oriented and those who were heterosexually oriented. However, until the early 1970s most theories about homosexuality discussed it in terms of mental disease or psychopathology. One reason for this was that psychiatrists obtained their data only from patients who had mental or emotional problems. By 1973, as mentioned earlier, the American Psychiatric Association had removed homosexuality from its list of mental diseases.

What Causes Differences?

Some scientists believe that a child's sexual orientation is determined before he or she is born. Dr. Lee Ellis, head of the Department of Sociology at Minot State University, Minot, North Dakota, pointed to the influence of sex hormones on an area of the brain called the hypothalamus.[4] The hypothalamus is organized differently for females and males and is believed by some to be a controlling factor in sexual orientation.

Dr. John Money, professor of medical psychology at Johns Hopkins University and Hospital School of Medicine in Baltimore, points to the evidence of anthropology and child development. This shows that most human beings are born with a bisexual potential. Whether this potential persists or changes to predominantly heterosexual or homosexual depends on influences that reach the brain through the senses, in particular the skin senses, vision, and hearing.

Other scientists refuse to offer any explanation of the causes of homosexual orientation until more conclusive evidence has been presented. Among these is Dr. June Reinisch of the Kinsey Institute at Indiana University.[5] According to Dr. Reinisch, scientists probably have a clearer idea about what *does not* cause most people to prefer a same-gender sexual partner. She has stated: "Children raised by gay or lesbian parents or couples are no more likely to be homosexual than are children raised by heterosexual parents."

23

In her review of studies on human sexuality, Dr. Reinisch saw no evidence that male sexual orientation is caused by a dominant mother or a weak father, or that female homosexual orientation is caused by girls choosing male role models. She found that under normal conditions parents have very little influence on their children's sexual orientation. Nor is it true, she contends, that young people who are seduced by older, same-gender persons in their youth will become homosexually oriented.

Sexual experiences for both the heterosexually oriented and the homosexually oriented are basically similar in childhood and adolescence. The only difference—and it is a major difference—is that those who are homosexually oriented find encounters with those of the opposite gender less satisfying.

The Sexual Freedom Factor

The sexual revolution of the late 1960s and the Gay Revolution that grew out of it encouraged a sexual freedom that for some gay men became boundless.[6] A Kinsey Institute survey of gay men in the 1970s revealed that almost half of those surveyed had had more than 500 sexual partners, and more than 90 percent had had at least 25. Most of these sexual encounters occurred with comparative or absolute strangers, oftentimes met in gay bars or bathhouses. This promiscuous behavior led inevitably to the spread of sexually transmitted diseases. On the other hand, the experiences of lesbians were more like those of women who were heterosexually oriented.

The rampant and widely reported promiscuity of gay

24

males has changed markedly, however, with the advent of the fatal disease AIDS, which spread quickly among promiscuous gay men. It is now the greatly feared scourge of both the homosexually and the heterosexually oriented. One positive result has been campaigns against promiscuous sexual activity and, for those who do have sexual encounters, campaigns promoting safe sex techniques.

Medical Attitudes Toward Homosexual Orientation

In spite of all the surveys and studies to the contrary, there persists in the minds of many people, including a substantial number of medical as well as religious professionals, the conviction that homosexual orientation is a sickness.[7] For instance, when the American Psychiatric Association removed homosexual orientation from its lists of mental disorders, it did so on the basis of a mail vote of its members. A clear majority, 5,854 or 60 percent, agreed with this decision. But there was still a substantial number, 3,810 or 40 percent, who did not. Further, when the International Classification of Diseases was published in 1980, homosexuality continued to be listed as a disease.

In a Kinsey Institute study published in 1978, known as the Bell and Weinberg Report, about 70 percent of those interviewed said they were reasonably satisfied with their homosexual orientation. Of the 30 percent who regretted their homosexual orientation, the strongest reason was the rejection they felt and experienced from society in general. Another major reason was the inability to produce children through lack of interest in heterosexual relationships.

Potential for Suicide

One of the disturbing results of the second Kinsey Institute survey was the finding that those with homosexual orientation, especially younger people, were far more likely to have attempted or seriously considered suicide. According to Bell and Weinberg, about 20 percent of gay males attempt suicide and another 20 percent think seriously about it. However, although not all of the suicide attempts or thoughts are related to homosexuality, about half of them are.

These facts led the researchers to conclude that about one in five young homosexuals is troubled enough about his or her homosexual orientation to think seriously about suicide, primarily because of social pressures and severe personal problems. All of these pressures intensify when sexual orientation becomes known to peers and family.

In his report on *Gay Male And Lesbian Youth Suicide*, therapist and program consultant Paul Gibson commented: "Gay and lesbian youth take tremendous risks by being open about who they are. You have to respect their courage." According to Gibson, they remain at high risk for suicidal feelings and behavior because of the pressures they face in conflicts with others about their homosexual orientation, especially with their peers and family.

"Openly homosexual youth are an affront to a society that would like to believe they don't exist," he stated.

26

"Our culture seems to have particular disdain for those gay youth who do not conform to gender expectations."

One solution to this problem is to include information and discussions about homosexual orientation in school courses that have discussions about other aspects of sexuality. The American Medical Association has a section on adolescent sexuality in the 1994 edition of its *Family Medical Guide*. In discussing homosexuality, the AMA points out that "homosexuals do not choose homosexuality any more than heterosexuals choose heterosexuality. Both 'just know' or are 'aware' of their sexual orientation from an early age. Reversing either orientation is difficult." It also acknowledges the fact that although psychiatrists differ in their approach to homosexuality, most consider it a normal variation of sexual behavior.

The AMA offers this advice to parents: "If your child tells you that he or she is homosexual, or if you think this may be true, you can get further information and support from an organization such as Parents and Friends of Lesbians and Gays (PFLAG)." Established in New York in 1973, PFLAG has more than two hundred chapters and contacts in the United States as well as active groups in Canada and six other countries. The national office is in Washington, D.C.

3

The Gay Revolution

Called by some the homosexual civil rights movement, the Gay Revolution, with its sustained drive for gay rights, seeks to put an end to all remaining laws that make homosexual acts between consenting adults illegal and punishable by fine and imprisonment.[1] It also seeks to end any discrimination against the homosexually oriented in employment, credit, housing, public accommodations and other areas of life.

In setting forth these goals, the movement is aimed at winning society's acceptance, or at the very least, society's tolerance of homosexual orientation and lifestyle. Several other attempts in this direction had been made in the 1920s and again in the 1950s, both in the United States and Europe. But the present drive, dating from the late 1960s, has been the most vigorously

Thousands of people march down Fifth Avenue in the annual Lesbian and Gay Pride Parade to mark the anniversary of the Stonewall Riot.

successful. It is still a formidable force more than a quarter of a century later.

The historic beginning of the gay rights movement has been timed almost to the instant: about three o'clock in the morning on Saturday, June 28, 1969, at a gay bar called the Stonewall Inn on Christopher Street in the Greenwich Village section of New York City. That is when the bar was raided by the police. Instead of passively accepting the raid, as in the past, the bar's two hundred or so patrons actively protested in a riot that lasted forty-five minutes. The rebellion continued on succeeding nights, sparked by protest rallies attended by gay patrons and sympathetic residents of the community.

Gay Pride Week

One direct result of the confrontation was the annual celebration of the "Stonewall" or "Christopher Street" riots in Gay Pride Week (or Gay and Lesbian Pride Week), held each year in late June in major cities across the country. These celebrations and other demonstrations began in an atmosphere created by a sexual revolution of young people, especially college students, against traditional values. There was the gender issue, with its controversies about male and female roles. Some young men let their hair grow long, wore necklaces, earrings, and colorful clothing. Some young women adopted the male macho look of short hair and army fatigues.

In a 1967 survey of young adults, more than half of the college freshmen interviewed said married women should not work. By 1984, this attitude was held by fewer than 25 percent. The number of women entering

31

the workforce, both married and single, continued to increase. So did the demand for equal rights, equal pay, and the opportunity to advance to top management levels. More and more women wanted the right to pursue professional careers, even those who were married and had children.

The availability of the birth control pill in the 1960s had opened the door to sexual freedom for both men and women. When the U.S. Supreme Court ruled that women had a legal right to abortions, women had won another freedom: the freedom to control their fertility, the freedom to decide when and if they wanted a child.

Political Activists

Conservative Christians had opposed the idea of homosexual orientation well before the gay rights movement began, denouncing it as sinful and evil. Any tolerance or acceptance advocated by gay rights groups and those sympathetic to their cause was denounced.

To fundamentalist Christians, homosexual orientation represented sex outside a family relationship. In the only acceptable relationship for them, a heterosexual relationship, a man and a woman complement each other not only sexually but spiritually.

Conservative Christians associated the gay rights movement with promiscuous sexual behavior, extramarital affairs, and a rejection of traditional gender roles for men and women; it represented a dangerous threat to the concept of family relationships. At times, the antihomosexual orientation extremists exceeded the bounds of reason or of Christian charity.[2]

When Anita Bryant, a popular singer and fervent

32

Christian fundamentalist, organized her "Save Our Children" crusade, she declared: "God puts homosexuals in the same category as murderers." The leader of the Moral Majority, Jerry Falwell, a fundamentalist Christian preacher, asked his followers to "stop the gays dead in their perverted tracks." One of his followers, Dan Wycoff of the Santa Clara, California, branch of the Moral Majority, announced on television his belief that homosexuality should be included with murder and other capital crimes "so the government that sits upon this land would be doing the executing."

Gay rights groups continue to fight against the hate and political suppression advocated by Christian extremists. Victories have been won in the political arena. For example, a female candidate who made no effort to hide the fact that she was lesbian was elected to the Massachusetts legislature in 1974. In the past two decades, gay men and women have been elected to political office in several states and held political appointments, including judgeships.

A milestone in the gay rights movement was the 1984 resolution by the U.S. Conference of Mayors calling for legal protection of the rights of gay males and lesbians at all levels of government. By 1986, antidiscrimination legislation or executive orders prohibiting some forms of discrimination had been passed or issued in seventy-six cities, counties, or states.

The Perils of "Coming Out"

In spite of progress made in achieving tolerance or acceptance of homosexual orientation, it is still a perilous step for a young person or an adult to "come out," in other words to tell family and friends that he or she is "gay." One teenager who took this step discussed it in a written statement to the author.

> I am sixteen years old, and I know that I am gay. I've known that I was somehow different from those around me for almost five years now. I've been hiding that side of me from myself and those around me since I learned I was "different." I was only recently able to "come out" to my immediate family and friends. I found that despite all of the misconceptions and prejudice surrounding homosexuality that my friends, all of them, were able to handle it and are still my friends. They know that it is a part of me and accept and love me no less than before they knew. If anything, I have gained immense respect from them and my family, and the important people around me, for my courage and ability to "come out" to them.

When word first spread through the school he attended that he was gay, there were some unpleasant reactions, including confrontations with some of his classmates and physical threats. But these faded with time. Some of the most stinging rebukes came as a result of religious convictions. He also admitted that it took him a long time to reconcile himself to the fact that he was gay. He had to be sure of this before he could admit the fact to any of his closest friends.

> More times than I can count I've been asked "What makes you think you're gay?" or "How do you know you are gay?" First of all, I don't "think" that I'm gay, I know I am. Secondly, my usual response to the question about knowing I'm gay is, "How do you know you aren't?" It makes them stop and think about it for a moment.

34

A marcher in a gay pride parade.

The only real difference between hetero- and homosexual people is that our attractions are different. That's it in its totality. I know I'm gay because I desire and pursue relationships with other men rather than with women. I'm not sexually attracted to members of the opposite sex. My sexual feelings are for members of my sex, and that is what is natural for me. I didn't become or choose to be that way. I just am. That's a part of who I am, but it is only a part, not all of who I am.

The "Gays in the Military" Controversy

For decades, the military refused to accept any man or woman who openly admitted that he or she was homosexually oriented. Those who were successful in keeping their sexual orientation a secret were able to serve without incident. But those who were suspected and investigated and proven to be homosexually oriented were dismissed from military service, oftentimes with a bad conduct or less than honorable discharge.

President Clinton met stiff opposition from the military and from many senators and representatives of both parties, Democrat and Republican, when he announced that he intended to make good on his campaign promise to lift the ban on gays serving in the military. As mentioned earlier, he was forced to temper his proposal to a policy of "Don't Ask, Don't Tell, Don't Seek, and Don't Flaunt." Military rules of conduct would still apply however. Any serviceman or -woman of homosexual orientation still ran the risk of military trial and discharge.

The Other Side of the Coin

For months, the "Gays in the Military" issue was a lead

President Bill Clinton meeting with the Joint Chiefs of Staff at the White House in 1993.

story in newspapers and magazines throughout the country, as the nation's opinion-makers sought to resolve the issue either by accepting or rejecting the stand President Clinton had taken. Many conservative publications were strongly opposed to any softening of the military's anti-homosexual orientation policy. E. L. Patullo, retired former director of the Center for Behavioral Sciences at Harvard University, wrote in the March 1, 1993 issue of the *National Review*:

> If, on average, gays are less martial than straights, it is only because one segment of the gay community, has, traditionally, cultivated an effeminacy that disdains soldierly virtues. Many gays, certainly, are as courageous, and as willing and able to fight, as are straights.
>
> With homosexuality out of the military closet they would be no more likely to be security risks than anyone else. Why, then, does the military oppose Bill Clinton's decision to admit homosexuals into the armed forces?

He then answered his own question by pointing out some of the problems created by the sexual urges experienced by both heterosexuals and homosexuals, how they are similar, and how they are different. Patullo contended that although straight men and women are powerfully motivated to have sex with each other, gay men and women are motivated not just to have sex with gays of the same gender but with any person of the same gender to whom they may be attracted.

> Gays are as able as the rest of us to control their libido, which means that—like the rest of us—they often need a bit of help in doing so. The intensity of the sexual urge—gay or straight—is so strong

that society recognizes that it is sensible, even in this permissive era, to maintain some barriers between potential sex partners.

If men and women who are homosexually oriented were openly admitted into military service, he argued, those barriers would no longer exist.

The infamous Tailhook '91 affair offers a strong corollary to Patullo's contention about the ability of gay men and women to control their sexual urges. The 1991 annual meeting of the Tailhook Association, whose aim is to facilitate contacts between naval officers and civilian contractors, was held in Las Vegas. It may have enhanced contacts between the navy and industrial suppliers, but it also produced a scandal that one courageous woman officer refused to suppress.

In an article titled, "Uncle Sam Doesn't Want You!" in the September 23, 1993 *New York Review of Books,* Robert Stone, who had spent a brief stint in the U.S. Navy as a young man, described the ninety separate "indecent assaults" perpetrated by scores of young men, presumably of heterosexual orientation, "who happened to be naval and marine corps aviators."[3] In a "gauntlet" planned by the male officers, women including many young female officers and navy wives, "were lured into a narrowing corridor, surrounded, and then generally felt up, pinched on the breasts and buttocks, and otherwise groped and insulted."

According to Stone's account, some women dismissed the drunken aviators as "jerks," but many others were terrified and feared for their safety. One of the sexually harassed, Admiral's Aide Paula Coughlin, complained first to her boss, Admiral John W. Snyder, Jr.

But when no action was taken, she took her story to the press, thus opening the scandal to full public view.

In detailing the scandal and the reluctant investigation that followed, Stone drew a parallel with the enthusiasm of the Naval Investigative Service (NIS) in uncovering service men and women of homosexual orientation. The Tailhook '91 affair, he said, gave the NIS "an unaccustomed exercise on the straight side of the street." In a wry final shot at the end of his article he recounted, "And two of the officers who had their buttocks pinched and fondled were men."

Conduct Unbecoming

In 1993, a book about men and women of homosexual orientation serving in the U.S. military was published and became an immediate best-seller. The author, Randy Shilts, was gay, and his book, *Conduct Unbecoming: Lesbians and Gays in the U.S. Military, Vietnam to the Persian Gulf,* put a glaring spotlight on the abuses of constitutional rights and other injustices meted out to servicemen and -women discovered to be homosexually oriented.[4] Chief among those cited for abuse by Shilts was the Naval Investigative Service. He wrote: "Call the NIS and tell them you've got a dead body and you think the murderer was homosexual and the agents will be there in thirty seconds."

Shilts also documented the military's ability to "look the other way" when a prospective enlistee admitted he was homosexually oriented, if there was an unusual demand for recruits. This happened during the Vietnam War in the 1960s. The experience of Perry Watkins, an

Randy Shilts, author of *Conduct Unbecoming: Gays and Lesbians in the U.S. Military, Vietnam to the Persian Gulf.*

African American from Tacoma, Washington, was cited.[5]

In May, 1968, Perry Watkins told his draft board that he was gay, but they ignored him. This prompted Shilts's sarcastic comment: "There were no gay blacks of military age in Tacoma the year of the Tet Offensive." Watkins was trained for military service, liked it, and served with distinction, attaining the rank of sergeant. He developed a talent for doing female impersonations at Army shows and they became a hit routine. Whenever he was given a form to fill out that asked him to reveal his sexual preference he stated that he was gay. This went on for sixteen years until finally, during the years of the Reagan presidency, his status was challenged and he was discharged.

Perry Watkins did not take the discharge lying down. He sued. In 1990, the U.S. Court of Appeals ordered his reinstatement, but the military appealed the decision. Finally, in November of that year, twenty-three years after he had first appeared before the Tacoma, Washington draft board, the U.S. Supreme Court decided in favor of Watkins and ordered the military to give him all the pay and allowances due him.

Results of the Rand Study

The same year that Shilts's book was published, the results of an independent study commissioned by Defense Secretary Les Aspin was made public. The study, made by the Rand Corporation, a research group often consulted by the Defense Department, recommended that gays be permitted to serve openly in the military.[6] The study did state that problems could occur, but declared that there was ample reason to believe that military personnel of both heterosexual and homosexual orientation could work together effectively.

Many critics of the President's policy of allowing gays to serve in the military exaggerated the potential problems, according to Rand Corporation researchers. The study also expressed the opinion that few gay military personnel would be likely to make their sexual orientation public. The great majority, as heretofore, would "stay in the closet."

The executive order issued by President Clinton in 1993 ended the practice of questioning recruits and service personnel about their sexual orientation. It also clearly stated that homosexual orientation would not prevent anyone from serving in the military. Further, military commanders or police and security units could not conduct investigations whose sole purpose was to determine someone's sexual orientation.

Even though military personnel continued to be at risk in military courts if they publicly declared that they were homosexually oriented, the trend in civilian courts was quite the opposite. In 1987, Joseph Steffan, a cadet at the U.S. Naval Academy, was forced to resign under pressure when he admitted he was homosexually oriented when asked the question by a superior officer. Six years later, in 1993, a panel of judges in a federal appeals court in Washington, D.C., ordered his reinstatement at the U.S. Naval Academy.[7]

It was the third such decision that year. In the unanimous opinion of the three-judge panel, Judge Abner Mikva wrote: "America's hallmark has been to judge people by what they do and not by who they are."

The Dissenters

As with all other issues in regard to homosexual orientation, however, there is a substantial segment who refuse to tolerate or accept homosexual orientation as legally legitimate. They see any step toward toleration or acceptance as immoral and a threat to the public good. The "gays in the military" issue is one more example of this.

Opponents of any relaxation of military policy have been blatant in their condemnation. One critic pointed out that many young people in military service, both men and women, are still in the process of discovering their sexual identity even into early adulthood. For such young people, the critic warned, it would be a dangerous course from a sexual orientation point of view for them to join a military service that made no distinction between those who were gay and those who were straight or heterosexually oriented.

Declared sociologist E. L. Patullo, "The intimate, around-the-clock conditions of barracks life will put them—as compared to their civilian counterparts—at increased risk of gravitating toward primary homosexuality."

Concerns were also raised about the effects on morale of allowing lesbians and gays to serve with the heterosexually oriented. This would make military life more attractive to men and women who are homosexually oriented. Also, it would increase the potential for the disruptive effects of those who would actively seek support of gay rights in other areas of life. This would include the right of two persons of the same gender to live together and to be entitled to the same rights and privileges as a heterosexual couple, husband and wife, who serve in the military.

Some critics, like Patullo, said the morale factor might not be critical in all branches of military service. But it could be seriously damaging to the morale of combat troops, who must operate under strict discipline, especially when under fire. Patullo stated: "Only those too young to have experienced amorous love, or too old to remember its power, can deny its potential for disrupting working relationships."

In spite of the fears and doubts raised by Patullo and others about the feasibility of gays and heterosexuals being able to work together without emotional conflicts, the records of past wars speak for themselves. As one observer has pointed out, unidentified numbers of men and women of homosexual orientation have served in the armed forces not only without incident but with distinction. The same working relationships exist in civilian life. There, as in the military, the majority of gays keep their sexual identities private and do the jobs they were trained to do.

45

4

Religious Views

A typical fundamentalist Christian response to homosexual orientation is that the man or woman with this orientation may be loved as a person, but their homosexual lifestyle can never be accepted. Even if that person is living with someone of the same gender in a monogamous relationship and they are faithful to each other, an ideal shared by heterosexuals, this would not make the relationship respectful. According to the fundamentalist view, such behavior in and of itself is sinful. No one should pretend otherwise. As one devout fundamentalist expressed it, "Don't lie to homosexuals."[1]

This particular person was no stranger to those with homosexual orientation. His best friend was gay and so was a very close family member. Both of these men he loved as human beings, but always with the reservation that their lifestyles were morally unacceptable. It was because he cared about their physical and spiritual well-being that he wanted them to know why he could not accept their lifestyle.

In his rejection of homosexual orientation and the homosexual lifestyle, this man admitted he had sometimes been guilty of homophobic name-calling, lapsing occasionally into demeaning language, referring to them as "queers" and "faggots." He had also been guilty of viewing them as stereotypes rather than as individual, unique human beings. But like many fundamentalists who want to treat all humans, including those with homosexual orientation, with compassion, he wondered just how far he could honestly stretch his compassion without descending into righteous anger and rejection.

He spoke of his relationship with his son who would prefer that he love him without criticizing actions he disapproved of, in particular those that would be harmful to him. But this was something he could not do. For example, he refused to let his son go to a dance club known to be patronized by young people who use drugs and who were prone to violent behavior, even though he knew that by so doing he had made his son angry with him. The point he made was that he cared enough about his son not to let him fall prey to evil influences. He knew he was doing the right thing by his son.

In the same way, he refused to accept the homosexual lifestyle because he honestly believed it is wrongful behavior in God's eyes. Like many others opposed to the homosexual lifestyle, he considered it unhealthy behavior. He asked:

> Is it homophobic to want my homosexual friend
> and family member to enjoy good health and a

Ed Dobson, pastor of Calvary Church, Grand Rapids, Michigan, a leader in the Christian fundamentalist Moral Majority in the 1980s. He later became involved in a ministry to people with AIDS.

lifestyle free of guilt? Is it wrong to report the medical truth that anal intercourse and other more intrusive practices used by male homosexuals are unhealthy, perhaps deadly? . . . Virtually every other segment of society is telling the homosexual it is okay to engage in homosexual behavior. Is it really our role to focus solely on acceptance of the person without recognizing the sinfulness of the behavior?

The Biblical Record

According to religious fundamentalists, there are many references to homosexual behavior in the Bible, and in every instance it is condemned. As evidence of this, they point to chapter and verse in the books of Leviticus, Deuteronomy, and Genesis in the Old Testament and to Romans, Corinthians, and Timothy in the New Testament.[2] Both Leviticus (18:22 and 20:13) and Deuteronomy (23:18) references, they claim, condemn homosexual behavior. In each case, they occur in discussions of God's disapproval of fertility cult practices in pagan communities adjoining the Israelite settlements.

In Genesis, Chapter 19, the story of Sodom and Gomorrah expresses God's outrage at the homosexual nature of the attempted gang rape, which symbolizes the general wickedness of the city in God's eyes. The reference in Romans, Chapter 1, is a condemnation of men and women of heterosexual orientation who engage in homosexual acts. This is cited as an example of rebellion against God by doing something that is sexually unnatural to them.

How Others View Biblical References

Some religious leaders in other Christian faiths, however, do not accept the fundamentalists' interpretation of Biblical references to homosexuality. For example, when Bishop John S. Spong of the Episcopal Diocese of Newark, New Jersey, was asked if scriptures in the Old and New Testaments objected to homosexuality, he protested that even if a person was to interpret the Bible literally he or she would not be able to build an ironclad case for condemnation.[3] For those who refuse to interpret the Bible literally there is no case at all, "nothing but prejudice born of ignorance that attacks people whose only crime is to be born with an unchangeable sexual predisposition toward those of their own sex."

According to Bishop Spong, even though the Biblical story of Sodom and Gomorrah is often cited as proof that the Bible condemns homosexuality, the real sin of Sodom was the unwillingness of men in that city to observe the laws of hospitality. They intended to insult the male stranger by forcing him to take the passive role in the sex act. At the same time, the Biblical narrative expresses approval of Lot's offer of his virgin daughters to satisfy the mob's sexual demands. Bishop Spong's response to this account was to raise the question, "Is this the word of the Lord?" In other words, was Lot acting as God wanted him to act by sacrificing his daughters to the lust of that mob of angry men?

The bishop agreed that Leviticus in the Hebrew scriptures condemns homosexual behavior, at least for males, but pointed out that the word used in Leviticus to describe homosexuality, "abomination," is the same

51

Roman Catholic priests hold mass on a sidewalk across from New York's St. Patrick's Cathedral. These priests are members of Cathedral Project Listen, a group supported by gays and lesbians.

word that is used to describe women's menstruation. He also protested against the misinterpretation of language whenever Paul is quoted as condemning homosexuality (in Romans, Timothy, and Corinthians). According to Bishop Spong, Paul regarded homosexuality as a punishment that God inflicted on those who worshipped idols because of their unfaithfulness to Him. In other words, homosexuality was not the sin but the punishment.

Bishop Spong, noting that Paul obviously did not approve of homosexual behavior, also noted that Paul and those who wrote the scriptures for the Old and New Testaments did not have an objective understanding of homosexual orientation. They were not only ignorant of facts but prejudiced as well. In defense of this view, he asked who today would share Paul's anti-Semitic attitude (hatred of Jews), his belief that the authority of the state was not to be challenged, or that all women ought to wear veils?

The Reverend C. Robert Nugent, a Catholic theologian who served as co-editor in 1988 of *The Vatican and Homosexuality*, expressed a somewhat less positive point of view about homosexual orientation and the homosexual lifestyle:

> Both Jewish and Christian scriptures do speak negatively of certain forms of same-gender (generally male) sexual *behavior* (not same-gender *love*), especially when associated with idol worship, lust, violence, degradation, prostitution, etc. Whether scriptures condemn all and every form of same-gender sexual expression *in and of itself* for all times, places, and individuals is the topic of serious theological and Biblical discussion and debate.
>
> Same-gender expressions of responsible, faithful

A protestor at a gay pride parade.

love in a covenanted relationship between two truly homosexually oriented people not gifted with celibacy is not something envisioned by scriptures. Whether this form of homosexuality violates biblical or anthropological principles of sexuality and personhood—especially in light of current scientific knowledge and human experience about the homosexual orientation—is a key issue facing the churches and religious groups today.

Fear of Promoting the Homosexual Lifestyle

What fundamentalist Christians and others opposed to the homosexual lifestyle fear most is not a scientific explanation of why a man or woman is homosexually oriented but promotion of the homosexual lifestyle, especially through school programs. Whenever attempts have been made by educational organizations and gay activist groups to promote acceptance of the homosexual lifestyle among school children, conservative and fundamentalist groups have been quick to meet the challenge and have sometimes been successful in overcoming it.

William Kilpatrick, a Boston College education professor and author of *Why Johnny Can't Tell Right from Wrong: Moral Illiteracy and the Case for Character Education*, has echoed the fears of many people that such so-called advances or liberalization play a harmful role in breaking down young people's ideas of what normal, proper, and acceptable behavior is.[4] Such an attempt to change traditional family values has been characterized as a "very slippery slope." Yet in spite of threats to their point of view, traditional conservatives have held their own in many school districts.

55

A Christian group led by the Traditional Values Coalition of Anaheim, California, was successful in deleting measures in proposed health education legislation that, in their opinion, went far beyond reasonable limits of a fair discussion of homosexuality.[5] In their view, it amounted to promotion of the homosexual lifestyle, and they made some drastic changes.

Only Three References to Homosexuality

In the discussion of guidelines for children in kindergarten through senior year in high school, only three references to homosexuality were permitted. The statement that gay and lesbian young people often experience difficulty in coming to terms with their sexual identity was eliminated. Also deleted was a definition of "family" that included households headed by couples of the same gender. The revised discussion framework stated that:

> Children develop best when they live in a stable environment with their mother and father who provide consistent love, support, and direction. However, children from nontraditional families can also develop successfully; given the variety of nontraditional families in contemporary society.

The emphasis on the potential for suicide among gay and lesbian students in response to verbal and physical abuse by peers, family, and others was also eliminated. In its place was a statement to the effect that among those students at higher risk to commit suicide are those who are homosexually oriented along with perfectionists, loners, previous attempters, and the severely depressed who have been sexually abused or molested.

Fear of AIDS

The spread of the sexually transmitted disease AIDS—Acquired Immune Deficiency Syndrome—among teenagers who are sexually active has made it vital for schools to provide all students with information about how this fatal disease is contracted. AIDS is caused by a virus that attacks the body's immune system. This makes the body easy prey to a host of diseases, including certain forms of pneumonia and cancer. The AIDS disease originated among men and women in Central Africa. When it was first identified in the United States in 1982, however, it had become epidemic among gay males. Also among the earliest to be diagnosed were addicts who injected illegal drugs into their veins and shared needles with other addicts suffering from AIDS, and hemophiliacs (males who bleed easily and need transfusions to replace blood lost as the result of injury or surgery) who had unintentionally been given blood infected with the AIDS virus.

By far the greatest number affected early on, however, were gay males. This brought a strong public reaction against those who were homosexually oriented, especially those whose lifestyle was promiscuous, that is, involving a great number of sex partners. In many people's minds, AIDS became a "gay men's disease," and for many fundamentalist Christians it was God's punishment to them for sinful behavior and a sinful lifestyle.

As the AIDS epidemic grew in alarming numbers, however, the number of heterosexually oriented men and women infected also grew. The disease also began to make inroads among the teenage population. With this development, a campaign was proposed by the U.S.

Demonstrators gather to urge the government to improve healthcare and AIDS research.

Surgeon General and many other health leaders and organizations, among them gay activist groups, to teach "safer sex" techniques to children in middle grades and high school. For example, the use of condoms in sexual intercourse, whether heterosexual or homosexual, was heavily promoted.

The mandate called for teaching safe sex practices not only to the heterosexually oriented, but also to those who were bisexually or homosexually oriented so that all known sexual practices would be covered. The idea of informing students about the spectrum of sexual practices, especially homosexual ones, appalled many parents and anyone opposed to the homosexual lifestyle. They were firmly against any educational program that would directly or indirectly show acceptance of a lifestyle they abhorred.

Commented one critic, "There is a difference between teaching tolerance of people and the dignity of other people and asking kids to accept certain behavior. Schools shouldn't be in the business of forcing children to accept lifestyles that the majority don't respect."[6]

Teaching Prevention

Those who promote AIDS Education Programs, however, have argued that the purpose is not to encourage sexual behavior among teenagers. After all, the surest way to avoid AIDS and any other sexually transmitted disease is through abstinence or celibacy, that is, by not engaging in sexual relations. That is an idea that many teenagers may want to uphold. However, studies have shown that one in seven teenagers has contracted a sexually transmitted disease through engaging in activities that have put them at risk.

Proponents have argued that AIDS prevention education is much more than a way of presenting information on how this dreaded disease is acquired through sexual activity, whether it be heterosexual, bisexual, or homosexual. Its purpose is to persuade young people to avoid behavior that may destroy their health and their lives.

5

The Charlie Howard Murder

Public and private views of people who are homosexually oriented and who accept a homosexual lifestyle for themselves can sometimes clash violently. This is what happened in Bangor, Maine, when a twenty-three-year-old gay man was murdered by three high school students.

On Saturday night, July 7, 1984, at about 10:30 P.M., Charlie Howard and a friend, twenty-year-old Roy Ogden, were walking in downtown Bangor, a city of 32,000 people. Howard was on the way to check his mailbox at the post office. They had just come from a meeting at the Universalist Church of an organization called Interweave, a support group for lesbians and gay males and straight or heterosexually oriented sympathizers. They were both casually dressed, Howard in blue jeans, a gray sweatshirt, and sneakers, Ogden in a T-shirt and army-style khaki pants.

Charlie Howard.

As they began to cross the State Street Bridge, which spans the 100-foot wide Kenduskeag stream, an approaching car slowed and came to a stop. The car was driven by sixteen-year-old Shawn Mabry. With him were two male friends, Dan Ness, seventeen, and Jim Baines, fifteen, and two female friends, Shawna Vanidestine, fifteen, and Jennifer Vafiades, seventeen. They were on the way to a party hosted by a classmate at Bangor High School.

Alleged "Sexual Comment"

Later, the group told police they stopped when they saw Howard because Baines said that he had made a "sexual comment" to him sometime in the past—an allegation later challenged by friends of Howard. All three young men got out of the car and shouted at Howard, "Hey, Fag!" Both Howard and Ogden had been chased so often by Bangor High School students in that area of town that they had found a secret hiding place under a staircase near the bridge. That's where they were fleeing toward until Howard tripped on a curb as he tried to run across the bridge.

Terrified, he fell hard on the sidewalk. He also began to experience a severe asthma attack, induced by his terror. As he was trying to get to his feet, he was suddenly surrounded by the three attackers. They pushed him back to the ground and began kicking him repeatedly. Then Baines yelled, "Over the bridge!" Baines and Ness picked Howard up and lifted him over the guardrail. Mabry pushed him down into the stream, twenty feet below, ignoring pleas from Howard, reported later to the police by his friend Ogden, of "No! No! I can't swim!"

As the three teenagers turned to leave, they yelled to Ogden who had witnessed the scene at a safe distance. They warned him not to get help or they'd take care of him, too. Then they got back in the car and continued on to the party, telling their friends when they got there that they had "jumped a fag and threw him in the stream."

Hoping to Get Help in Time

As soon as they left, Ogden, hoping to get help in time, raced down State Street until he found a fire alarm and pulled it. However, when the fire trucks and police arrived at the bridge there was no sign of Charlie Howard in the stream. As it flows through Bangor, the Kenduskeag stream is bordered on both sides by cement walls for about five hundred feet until the stream empties into the Penobscot River. There would be nothing for even a good swimmer to hold onto to pull him- or herself out of the stream. Charlie Howard was doomed the moment he was thrown into the stream because he could not swim.

Police found his bruised body several hundred feet downstream from the bridge, underwater, with a large eel wrapped around his neck. The coroner's verdict was death by drowning, complicated by a severe asthma attack.

When Charlie Howard's murder was reported the next morning, one of the teenagers, Dan Ness, turned himself in and confessed. The other two, Mabry and Baines, attempted to run away by hopping a freight train. Later, they gave up on this plan and were then arrested at their homes. The Maine attorney general's office declared that the state would ask the judge

Police searching for the body of Charlie Howard in Kenduskeag stream in Maine.

assigned to the case, Judge David Cox, to have them prosecuted as adults and push for a murder conviction. But Judge Cox disagreed and said they would be tried as juveniles. All three were released to the custody of their parents.

Who Was Charlie Howard?

Charlie Howard grew up in Portsmouth, New Hampshire, just across the Maine state line. Blond, slightly built, shy, gentle, and effeminate, his chronic asthma prevented him from playing many sports and he had never learned how to swim. Because of his effeminacy and gay orientation, he was shunned and taunted by his schoolmates. Because of this, he refused to attend his high school graduation. He didn't want his family and relatives to see him ridiculed by his peers.

A few years later he left Portsmouth, he told friends, so he would no longer be an embarrassment to his family, in particular his mother and an older brother who was a staff sergeant in the Army. For awhile, he lived with a man in Ellsworth, Maine, but when that didn't work out he decided to move to Bangor and seek work there. Eventually, he signed up for Workfare, a work assistance program that provided jobs for the unemployed. He rented a room in a boardinghouse behind the Unitarian church.

School Not Important to Them

According to the principal at Bangor High School, Dr. John Fahey, all three of the teenagers responsible for Charlie Howard's death were poor students and troublemakers. School wasn't important to them. He commented, "They didn't attend classes regularly, and they got in trouble."[1] Ness was described as an art student with good potential, but his grades that year were poor. Mabry liked the one-on-one contact sport of karate and was one of the star players in the city hockey league. But he didn't pass any of his courses and was ineligible to play on the school team. When all three were examined by a psychiatrist after their arrest, one of the major assessments was that they all had difficulty identifying with others and suffered from "self-centeredness."

The reactions of students at Bangor High School to the murder were mixed, reflecting to some degree a sharp division between acceptance and rejection of homosexual orientation. Two female students interviewed by a Boston newspaper several months after the tragedy were asked, "What would have happened if Charlie Howard had enrolled at Bangor High School?" One replied, "If I was gay I wouldn't have the guts to go to school here." The other joined in, "I'd move to another continent."[2]

Evidently the efforts of the Bangor School Committee to address the issue of tolerance had yet to make an impact on these and perhaps many other students and their parents. About a month and a half after Charlie Howard's murder, the committee had met and approved a statement of policy that was to be distributed at the opening of school to all faculty and staff. The statement read in part:

> Given the recent tragedy that has shaken our community, we are especially concerned about the rights of gays and lesbians to expect civility, and to

67

be free from harassment and physical abuse. We encourage our teachers to air these issues in their classrooms, where appropriate to the subject matter. We support our administrators and staff in their reprimand of intolerance in all its forms.[3]

"Not A Martyr"

The reaction of the *Bangor Daily News* to Charlie Howard's murder reflected many of the attitudes and opinions of those firmly opposed to the homosexual lifestyle. A major editorial published in its Saturday–Sunday edition, July 14–15, a week after the murder, acknowledged the tragedy of Charlie Howard's murder but devoted most of its space to the political implications.

Citing Howard "as a rather flamboyant homosexual" whose friends and sympathizers considered a victim of extreme homophobia (fear of homosexuals) and prejudice, the editors refused to accept their conclusion that his death was a form of martyrdom to irrational hatred and bigotry. This is stated in the editorial's headline, "Not A Martyr."[4]

Nor did they agree that a gay rights bill should be passed by the state legislature making it illegal to discriminate against gay males and lesbians in jobs, housing, marriage, adoptions, "and other opportunities available to most people in the community." According to the editorial, those in favor of the homosexual lifestyle and gay rights wanted to change the "somewhat tolerant but certainly not accepting" attitude of society by legislating against it.

Rejecting both points of view, the editorial endorsed a middle ground. There was no widespread sentiment for a campaign to suppress homosexuals who were law-abiding, it stated. On the other hand, neither was there "significant" interest in making Howard a martyr. In fact, the editors were strongly opposed to using his tragic death as an excuse to pass laws that would single out men and women of homosexual orientation for special treatment.

Rejection of Gay Rights Laws

The editors reminded readers that four times in the past the state legislature had rejected proposed gay rights laws. They were not aware of any proposed law that could have prevented Charlie Howard's murder. The editorial concluded:

> The controversy generated by a reintroduction of gay rights legislation will only serve to polarize further the people of the state, antagonizing those who perceive it to be threatening and destructive, frustrating those who misguidedly see it as progress, and alienating the majority of Maine voters, who firmly believe such laws are unwise, unnecessary, and self-defeating.

Readers Respond

The editorial in the *Bangor Daily News* provoked a heavy onslaught of letters to the editor in that paper and many others throughout Maine, as well as in newspapers in other states where the murder had been reported. Strong opinions were expressed both for and against the editorial, especially by those who considered themselves deeply religious. One man, accepting Howard's death as tragic, nonetheless resented any attempt to use it to support the legitimacy of the homosexual lifestyle. In response to one

A gay pride march in Bangor, Maine, in July 1994.

letter from a Catholic priest in Old Town, a nearby city, who had asked for tolerance, this man declared:

> I pray to God the members of St. Joseph's Church in Old Town have the wisdom to see the error of this teaching. The Bible clearly shows the only way for homosexuals to attain God's kingdom is to confess their sin and change their ways. . . . Only when the homosexual is ready to repent will I welcome him or her to worship the Lord with me.

Probably the most extreme response was reported in the newsletter of the All Souls Unitarian Church in Augusta, Maine, the state capital. A minister from South Carolina had written to the Reverend Douglas Strong, minister of All Souls Unitarian Church, July 11, four days after Charlie Howard's murder:

> I cannot understand why you are so upset over the death of a pervert. The only good thing to be said about a pervert is that he can not reproduce. I wish every pervert in the world would contract AIDS. That way we would be rid of all these creeps.[5]

Openly Gay and Lesbian Role Models

A man writing to the editor of the *Boston Globe* wondered if justice would be done, recalling that a recent antigay attack in Boston had resulted in a $200 fine, and a brutal knife assault against a gay person in Washington, D.C., resulted in the perpetrator being let off with probation until age twenty-one. He also pointed to the 1978 murders in San Francisco of Mayor George Moscone and the openly gay Supervisor Harvey Milk, which resulted in a mere five-year prison term for the killer, former Supervisor Dan White.[6]

One solution to antigay violence, the man wrote, is

to meet the need for "openly gay and lesbian role models. If the Bangor teenagers had known that some of their most respected teachers, athletic heroes, or movie stars are gay, would they have been so quick to attack Charles Howard?"

This point was underscored in a news story in the *Bangor Daily News* in the Wednesday edition immediately following the murder. Bearing the headline, "Fear of Gays Widespread, Psychologists Say," the story highlighted interviews with area psychologists, including Dr. Lee Nickoloff of the Cutler Health Center at the University of Maine at Orono. She declared that one way to counter homophobia is to make conscious contact with them. Too many lesbians and gay men are ignored or "invisible" to the great majority who are heterosexually oriented.[7]

Also interviewed was Dr. Marvin Ellison, professor of Christian ethics at Bangor Theological Seminary, where he taught a course on sexuality. Dr. Ellison said that another way to correct the problem is for homophobic persons to start working on their own fears, uncertainties, and anxieties about sexuality. The clergy could help, he said, through education, advocating civil rights for gays and lesbians, and making them feel welcome in their churches and free to talk about their concerns and problems.

The Verdict

The Charlie Howard murder case was not resolved until three months after the event. Two of the teenagers who had been released to the custody of their parents, Ness and Baines, had caused no problems, but Mabry had

The teenagers accused of the Howard murder in the custody of
police.

gone to a rock concert and got into a fistfight with another concertgoer.

The lawyer representing the state, Assistant Attorney
General Thomas Goodwin, was willing to settle the case
through plea bargaining. The murder charge was
dropped and in place of a trial the teenagers agreed to
plead guilty to the lesser charge of manslaughter. Judge
Cox gave them an "indeterminate" sentence to the
Maine Youth Center. Officials at the center would determine their eligibility for parole. Under the Maine
Juvenile Code they would have to be released on or before their twenty-first birthdays.

Homosexuality
and the Law

Long before the Sexual and Gay Revolutions of the late 1960s and early 1970s, attempts had been made to improve the legal status of persons of homosexual orientation, but with little success. For the first six decades of the twentieth century, sexual relations between those of the same gender, referred to in legal language as homosexual acts, were illegal in every state of the Union.

The laws against such acts were often labeled antisodomy laws. These acts were also illegal in many states if committed by those of heterosexual orientation.

Antisodomy laws were first enacted in the United States in the latter part of the nineteenth century, but few cases have been brought to court. Nevertheless, the people who were tried and found guilty were sometimes severely punished.[1] For example, during World War II, a man in Brooklyn, New York, who had helped the government capture German spies was taken to court for operating a male homosexual place of entertainment. Despite his wartime service to his country, he was convicted and made to serve a full twenty-year prison sentence. In the mid-1950s, some of the men convicted in a homosexual scandal in Boise, Idaho, were sent to prison for long terms. One man was sentenced to prison for life.

First Step Taken in 1961

By the late 1950s, however, the movement to decriminalize antisodomy laws and to permit sexual contact in private between consenting adults of homosexual orientation was gaining momentum. In 1961, the first step was taken in Illinois where a new penal code was enacted. It declared that private homosexual acts between consenting adults were no longer a crime.[2]

Since then, many other states have followed suit, but not all. As of 1994, there were still twenty-one states in which antisodomy laws were in effect, including those laws that applied to heterosexuals as well as homosexuals. Many attempts have been made to overturn these laws, with varying degrees of success. One famous case that was taken all the way to the U.S. Supreme Court involved the state of Georgia.

The year was 1986 and the case was docketed as *Bowers* v. *Hardwick*.[3] It began with a police raid at the home of Michael Hardwick, who was found in bed with another adult male. He was immediately charged with violating a Georgia antisodomy law that criminalized any sex act involving the mouth or anus of one person and the sex organs of another. Classified as a felony, if convicted, a person could be sentenced from one to twenty years in prison.

Refused to Accept Charge As Legal

Refusing to accept the police action and charge as legal, Hardwick filed suit in a federal district court, claiming that the Georgia law was unconstitutional. When the district court dismissed his claim without a trial, he took his case to the Circuit Court of Appeals. This time, his lawyer attached copies of a brief filed by the American Psychological Association and the American Public Health Association in a recent gay rights case in New York.

By a two-to-one vote the Appeals Court held that the Georgia statute interfered with the fundamental right of citizens to engage in private, intimate, consensual conduct. It also did three other things. It ordered the district court to hold a trial to hear Hardwick's claim. It required the state to prove that it had a compelling interest in regulating private sexual conduct between consenting adult males. And it ordered the state to prove that the antisodomy statute was the most narrowly drawn means of safeguarding that interest.

Instead of acting on the Appeals Court's ruling, however, the state was successful in getting the U.S. Supreme Court to review it, with favorable results from the state's point of view. However, the U.S. Supreme Court's decision in favor of the state was not unanimous, with five justices in favor and four opposed.

"Such Laws Have Ancient Roots"

The Court's majority vote reversed the Appeals Court decision. It stated that the U.S. Constitution does not

confer on those who are homosexually oriented a fundamental right to engage in sodomy. Upholding Georgia's
antisodomy statute, the majority declared that "such
laws have ancient roots." Such conduct, they said, was
criminalized under common law and forbidden by the
laws of the thirteen original states when they ratified the
Bill of Rights. In a concurring opinion, Chief Justice
Warren Burger declared that the prohibition of same-
gender sexual conduct was firmly rooted in Judaeo-
Christian moral and ethical standards.

The majority decision was tempered somewhat by
Justice Lewis F. Powell, Jr., who had voted with the majority. He stated that if the defendant, Hardwick, was
convicted and imprisoned this might be a violation of
the 8th Amendment to the U.S. Constitution's cruel and
unusual punishment clause.

Right to be Left Alone

The four dissenting justices firmly declared that the case
was not a question about any citizen's right to engage in
homosexual sodomy. Far overriding this issue, they
agreed, was the most comprehensive of all citizens'
rights: the right to be left alone. They also pointed out
that homosexual orientation is not considered a disease
but part of an individual's personality.

They took issue with the argument that antisodomy
laws are justified because they are based on the moral
and religious codes of certain religious groups. There is a
wide difference, they claimed, between laws that protect
public sensibilities and those that enforce private
morality.

In spite of the Supreme Court's five-to-four vote in

Hundreds of gay rights activists demonstrate against a Supreme Court decision that upheld a Georgia law making sodomy a crime.

favor of Georgia's antisodomy law, however, the case was never brought to trial. The state dropped all charges against Hardwick.

Sexual Conduct in Texas

Unlike Georgia's antisodomy law, which applies to all persons regardless of their sexual orientation, the antisodomy law in Texas was written to apply only to those who are homosexually oriented. In 1992, six years after the U.S. Supreme Court made its decision upholding Georgia's law, the Texas statute was challenged by a group of professionals representing the American Psychological Association (APA), the National Association of Social Workers (NASW), and the Texas chapter of NASW.[4]

They accused the statute of being arbitrary and unjust and a violation of constitutional guarantees of equal protection under the law. The Texas law criminalizing homosexual conduct described it as any act involving the genitals of one person and the mouth or anus of another person of the same gender.

In a brief comprising forty-two pages of information, arguments, and citations, the group challenging the law pointed to studies that showed that 90 percent of married and unmarried heterosexual couples had engaged in oral-genital sex. They cited another study that showed that about 80 percent of single men and women aged twenty-five to thirty-four had engaged in these acts.

The figures from studies of anal intercourse were much lower, although still substantial. One study of married couples revealed that 25 percent of those under thirty-five years of age had engaged in anal intercourse in the year preceding the study.

Denial of Equal Protection

"Just as it is important to many heterosexual relationships, oral and anal sex are among the primary forms of sexual expression available to gay people," the challengers declared. Denying those persons of homosexual orientation the right to express themselves sexually and to enjoy the same sexual freedom available to those of heterosexual orientation, they stated, is not only unfair, it is an unconstitutional denial of their right to equal protection under the law.

They also argued that criminalizing homosexual acts does not in any way prevent or limit homosexual orientation. Studies have shown that the incidence of this sexual orientation (one estimate is 3 percent of the adult population) appears to remain constant throughout the United States, whether the laws in any particular state prohibit or permit homosexual acts.

The district court in which the brief was filed agreed that the Texas antisodomy law was unconstitutional. That decision went to the Court of Appeals, where the district court's ruling was upheld. However, the Texas Supreme Court disagreed. Under Texas law, for a statute to be declared unconstitutional, it is not enough to show that a citizen's personal rights are harmed. It must be shown that there is harm "to a vested property right." Because property rights were not an issue in the case, the district court did not have jurisdiction and was therefore instructed to dismiss the case.

Antigay Violence

One of the major organizations that documents incidents of antigay violence in the United States is the National Gay and Lesbian Task Force, founded in 1973 and headquartered in Washington, D.C. A report issued by the Task Force in 1987 showed an alarming rise in reported incidents, from 4,946 in 1986 to 7,008 in 1987. This was a 42 percent increase in incidents that ranged from verbal harassment to homicide.

According to the Task Force, antigay violence is motivated by irrational fear and hatred, encouraged by the fact that the haters consider gay men and women easy targets. They are often unable or unwilling to fight back in many communities because of the indifference and lack of protection from police and other local authorities.

Risk of Exposing Themselves

In states where antisodomy laws remain on the books gay people are reluctant or afraid to report crimes against them. By doing so, they risk exposing themselves to authorities as persons whose sexual orientation is homosexual. This can make them liable to prosecution.

A sampling of incidents reported to the Task Force in 1987 illustrates the plight of gay people even in states where homosexual acts have been de-criminalized. In Long Beach, California, three young men assaulted a gay man with AIDS, breaking his hip and causing other injuries. The attackers were arrested, but the police released them when they learned that the victim had AIDS.

In San Francisco, a man of heterosexual orientation

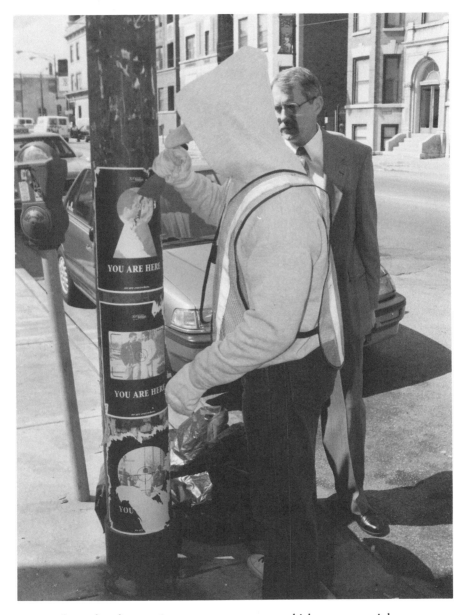

A work release prisoner scrapes posters which promote violence against gays from a light pole in Chicago.

became a murder victim because his assailant mistakenly perceived him to be gay. He was a tourist, unfamiliar with the section of the city he happened to be in. He was on his way to a dance club when a man accosted him, called him "faggot" and "fruit" and stabbed him in the face and abdomen. The victim staggered for several blocks and then collapsed and died two hours later. According to the police report, there was no evidence that he had in any way provoked the attack. He was just "at the wrong place at the wrong time."

An incident in Philadelphia involved a lesbian at a local bar. She was accosted by a man who tried to pick her up. When she told him she wasn't interested because of her sexual orientation, the man dragged her out of the bar onto the sidewalk where he proceeded to beat her up. She was later treated for lacerations that required stitches at a hospital emergency room.

An Incident Involving Federal Government

The following year, 1988, the American Civil Liberties Union documented the first antigay violence case filed against the federal government: *Anderson and Grubb* v. *Branen.*[5] Marc Anderson and his companion, Jeffrey Grubb, claimed they were viciously assaulted by three agents of the U.S. Drug Enforcement Administration (DEA), Dennis Branen, Ross Kindestin, and Ed Winiefski, after a minor traffic incident. Anderson and Grubb accused the agents of abusing them verbally with a barrage of antigay epithets as well as assaulting them physically. When the police arrived on the scene, the DEA agents had Anderson and Grubb arrested and charged with various crimes. The charges were later dropped.

However, two years later, in October 1990, a civil case against the DEA agents was entered on behalf of Anderson and Grubb in federal district court in New York. The plaintiffs claimed that Anderson's and Grubb's civil rights had been violated when the agents used excessive force during the arrest. When the case went to trial in April 1993, the jury became deadlocked, unable to agree on a verdict. The government moved to dismiss the case. When that motion was denied, an appeal was made to the Second Circuit Court. It was then scheduled for retrial at a later date.

Liberties of All Citizens Threatened

Much antigay violence, both verbal and physical, goes unreported because too many teenagers and adults are reluctant to seek the protection guaranteed to all citizens under the U.S. Constitution. No matter how many attacks are made and reported, however, as the National Gay and Lesbian Task Force has pointed out, the violation of any citizen's rights puts the rights of all others in jeopardy. The Task Force declared:

> Regardless of the actual extent of antigay violence, *any* attack based on sexual orientation is intended to violate and isolate not just the victim, but *all* lesbian and gay people. As with other crimes motivated by prejudice, antigay harassment and violence are forms of terrorism aimed at depriving lesbian and gay citizens of their basic human and civil rights—including their rights to freedom of speech, association, and assembly. As such, these acts strike at the very heart of our pluralistic society and ultimately threaten the liberties of all Americans.

85

Boycott Colorado, Inc., a group formed to protest the passage of Amendment 2, urges visitors to stay away from Colorado.

Antigay Legislation

There have been instances in which gay rights groups have been successful in securing protection against violence and discrimination in some cities and states. Some of these victories have later been defeated, however, by legal actions of those opposed to any tolerance or acceptance of homosexual orientation and lifestyles. One notorious instance took place in November 1992, when voters in Colorado approved Amendment 2. This amendment drastically changed the state's constitution, reversing years of efforts in all parts of the state in behalf of gay rights.[6] Amendment 2 firmly disavowed any form of protection of the rights of any citizen if based on his or her homosexual, lesbian, or bisexual orientation.

Defenders and promoters of gay rights took immediate action to stop the amendment from taking effect, and two years later their efforts were successful. By a decision of six-to-one, the Colorado Supreme Court declared the amendment unconstitutional. The amendment, they declared, singled out one form of discrimination, bias against homosexuals and bisexuals, and prevented them from attempting to redress any alleged wrongs against them by using the political process otherwise available to all United States citizens. As an editorial in the October 14, 1994 *New York Times* commented, the Colorado Supreme Court's decision "brilliantly affirms the right of all citizens, whatever their lifestyle preferences, to participate in lawmaking that affects their interests." It further commented, "The right to participate equally in the political process is as old as the Union."

7

Weighing Both Sides

The purpose of this book and all you have read so far is to help you understand why homosexual orientation is a controversial issue in America. With the information, arguments, and opinions expressed in the preceding chapters, you will be able to make up your own mind on the subject.

From the point of view of the proponents, those in favor of accepting homosexual orientation, progress has been made in eliminating discrimination in some areas, such as employment. However, employment of openly gay men and women has been strongly opposed in two key areas, teaching and military service.[1]

And yet, unquestioned progress has been made in the frankness with which sexual orientation is now discussed and also in eliminating harmful stereotypes (unfair or distorted images of a person or group of

89

persons). In general, people no longer believe that all gay men are effeminate, or are pedophiles (child molesters), or that all lesbians are masculine and aggressive.

Facts and Arguments in Favor

What follows is a summary of the main points in favor of accepting homosexual orientation as inevitable and valid for some men and women. One of the strongest arguments is that homosexual orientation has been a fact of life in all of recorded history, from the most ancient cultures to the present time. Homosexual orientation has persisted in spite of persecution and sometimes brutally savage repression.

In 1973, homosexual orientation was deleted from the list of mental illnesses by the American Psychiatric Association. Two years later, this action was endorsed by the American Psychological Association, which stated: "Homosexuality, per se, implies no impairment in judgment, stability, reliability, or general social or vocational capabilities."

So far, surveys by the Parents and Friends of Lesbians and Gays and other scientific studies have been unable to pinpoint the exact causes of heterosexual and homosexual orientation. But a predisposition toward homosexual, bisexual, or heterosexual orientation is present at birth in all boys and girls.

Some scientists believe that the influence of sex hormones on the hypothalamus area of the brain plays a major part in determining sexual orientation. Parental and other family relationships may have some influence, but they do not determine sexual orientation. Nor is it true that young people who are seduced by an older same-gender person will become homosexually oriented.

According to some religious leaders, even a literal interpretation of the Bible can not support an ironclad case for condemning homosexual orientation. Bishop John S. Spong of the Episcopal diocese in Newark, New Jersey, declared that there is no case for those who refuse to interpret the Bible literally. There is "nothing but prejudice born of ignorance that attacks people whose only crime is to be born with an unchangeable sexual predisposition toward those of their own sex."

Preventing Antigay Violence

What causes antigay violence, according to gay rights proponents, is ignorance and hate. Said one proponent, reacting to the Charlie Howard murder in Maine: "If the Bangor teenagers had known that some of their most accomplished teachers, athletic heroes, or movie stars are gay, would they have been so quick to attack Charles Howard?"

Another argument of those in favor of accepting homosexual orientation and putting an end to all forms of discrimination is that most informed people support their views. As evidence they point to the 1984 resolution of the U.S. Conference of Mayors which called for legal protection of gay rights at all levels of government.

When a gay person "comes out of the closet"—that is, tells family and friends that he or she is homosexually oriented—it is still a painful, fearful act. But more people have been willing now than in the past to accept it. Some politicians, athletes, movie stars, singers and other prominent people have had the courage to reveal their

Gay men and women and their parents march together in a show of
unity during a Los Angeles Gay and Lesbian Pride Parade.

homosexual orientation and this has encouraged others to do so.

One of the major arguments against making homosexual acts criminal is that many men and women who are heterosexually oriented perform the same acts with no threat of legal prosecution. Therefore, persons of homosexual orientation should have the same rights and are entitled to equal protection under the law. Another major argument against making homosexual acts criminal is that they do not in any way prevent or limit homosexual orientation. Further, people who are homosexually oriented cannot be forced to become heterosexually oriented.

Arguments Against

Among the most vehement opponents of accepting homosexual orientation are Christian fundamentalists, who claim there is ample testimony in both the Old and New Testaments of the Bible that God has condemned any form of homosexual orientation. As Christians, they can try to love the sinners and help them change their sinful ways. But they can never love or accept the sin.

As clear evidence of God's condemnation of homosexual acts, they cite chapter and verse in the books of Leviticus, Deuteronomy, and Genesis in the Old Testament and in Romans, Corinthians, and Timothy in the New Testament.

Acceptance of homosexual orientation in direct opposition to the Bible's condemnation is more than sinful in itself, they believe. It is also a threat to traditional family values. This is one reason why those who are most strongly opposed to accepting homosexual orientation fight any attempts to single out men and

93

women of homosexual orientation for what they consider to be "special treatment." This would include almost every item in the gay rights agenda, including the right to teach in public or tax-funded schools.

There is also the question of just how much tolerance of the homosexual lifestyle is justified and how much discussion of the homosexual lifestyle should be allowed in school educational programs. As one opponent declared: "There is a difference between teaching tolerance of people . . . and asking kids to accept certain behavior. Schools shouldn't be in the business of forcing children to accept lifestyles that the majority don't respect."

The Uncertainties of Science

Opponents also point to the lack of scientific proof that once a person believes he or she is homosexually oriented nothing can be done about it. In the Masters and Johnson study of fifty-four males and thirteen females who wanted help in changing their sexual orientation from homosexual to heterosexual, the success rate five years later was 72 percent.

There is also lack of agreement among mental health professionals. As opponents have pointed out, when members of the American Psychiatric Association voted to remove homosexual orientation from its list of mental illnesses in 1973, this decision was opposed by 3,810 members, which constituted 40 percent of the membership.

Probably the strongest objection to the acceptance of homosexual orientation is the threat it presents in many people's minds to the sanctity and preservation of the traditional family. For them, homosexual orientation represents sex performed outside a marital relationship. In their eyes, the only acceptable relationship or orientation is the heterosexual one, in which a man and a woman complement each other both sexually and spiritually.

The gay rights movement, for opponents, conjures up pictures of promiscuous sexual behavior and extra-marital affairs. It also poses an unacceptable rejection of traditional gender roles for men and women in the ideal Christian family relationship.

Making Up Your Own Mind

Now that you've read and reviewed the major arguments on both sides of this controversial issue, you have an important option. You have the freedom to make up your own mind, depending on what you believe to be true and what you believe will be best for the society in which you live.

Chapter Notes

Chapter 1

1. "Homosexual Rights Movement," *Encyclopaedia Britannica, Micropaedia Edition* (Chicago: Encyclopaedia Britannica, Inc., 1993), p. 31.

2. "Clinton Draws Ire of SBC," *Christianity Today* (July 19, 1993), p. 54.

3. Linda Garnets et al., "Issues in Psychotherapy with Lesbians and Gay Men—A Survey of Psychologists," *American Psychologist* (September 1991), p. 971.

4. Ibid.

5. Lee Ellis, *Why Is My Child Gay?* (Washington, D.C.: Federation of Parents and Friends of Lesbians and Gays, Inc., 1992).

Chapter 2

1. "Homosexuality," *Encyclopaedia Britannica, Micropaedia Edition* (Chicago: Encyclopaedia Britannica, Inc., 1994), pp. 249–251.

2. Michael Ruse, *Homosexuality, A Philosophical Inquiry* (New York: Basil Blackwell Ltd., 1988), pp. 1–20.

3. "Homosexuality," p. 251.

4. Lee Ellis, *Why Is My Child Gay?* (Washington, D.C.: Federation of Parents and Friends of Lesbians and Gays, Inc., 1992), pp. 6–7.

5. June Machover Reinisch, ed., *Masculinity/Femininity: Basic Perspectives* (New York: Oxford University Press, 1987), pp. 8–9.

6. Ruse, p. 10.

7. Ibid. pp. 203–235.

Chapter 3

1. "Homosexual Rights Movement," *Encyclopaedia Britannica, Micropaedia Edition* (Chicago: Encyclopaedia Britannica, Inc., 1994), pp. 30–31.

2. David F. Greenberg, *The Construction of Homosexuality* (Chicago: University of Chicago Press, 1988), pp. 455–481.

3. Robert Stone, "Uncle Sam Doesn't Want You!" *The New York Review of Books* (September 23, 1993), p. 20.

4. Randy Shilts, *Conduct Unbecoming: Lesbians and Gays in the U.S. Military, Vietnam to the Persian Gulf* (New York: St. Martin's Press, 1993), p. 335.

5. Ibid. pp. 61–65, 729–730.

6. Associated Press, "April Study, Just Out, Concludes Gays in Military OK," *Portland Press Herald* (August 27, 1993).

7. Bruce B. Auster, and Joseph P. Shapiro, "The Courts on Gays," *U.S. News and World Report* (November 29, 1993), p. 12.

Chapter 4

1. "Don't Lie to Homosexuals," *Christianity Today* (May 17, 1993), p. 17.

2. Stanton L. Jones, "The Loving Opposition," *Christianity Today* (July 19, 1993), pp. 20–25.

3. Episcopal Bishop John S. Spong, *Is Homosexuality A Sin?* (Washington, D.C.: Federation of Parents and Friends of Lesbians and Gays, Inc., 1992), pp. 11–12.

4. William Kilpatrick, quoted in "Homosexual Rights Go to School," *Christianity Today* (May 17, 1993), p. 71.

5. Ibid. pp. 71–72.

6. Ibid. p. 72.

Chapter 5

1. Michael Kranish, "A Clash of Lifestyle, A Death in Bangor," *Boston Globe* (August 13, 1984), pp. 17–18.

2. Peter Canellos, "A City and Its Sins," *The Boston Phoenix* (November 13, 1984), p. 28.

3. Sue Hyde, "Bangor School Committee Addresses Homophobia," *Gay Community News* (September 15, 1984).

4. "Not A Martyr," *Bangor Daily News*, editorial (July 14–15, 1984).

5. Dr. C. Paul Jackson, *All Souls Unitarian Church Newsletter* (August 1984), p. 2.

6. Jonathan Handel, "Gay Bias Encouraged by Attitudes of Elected and Moral Leaders," *Boston Globe* (August 13, 1984).

7. Jean Curran, "Fear of Gays Widespread, Psychologists Say," *Bangor Daily News* (July 11, 1984), pp. 1, 3.

Chapter 6

1. David F. Greenberg, *The Construction of Homosexuality* (Chicago: University of Chicago Press, 1988), pp. 455–456.

2. Ibid.

3. *Bowers* v. *Hardwick*, American Psychological Association Amicus Curiae Briefs, "Further Lesbian and Gay Male Civil Rights," (September 1991), pp. 952–953.

4. *The State of Texas* v. *Linda Morales, Tom Doyal, Patricia Cramer, Charlotte Taft, and John Thomas*, Brief for Amici Curiae, American Psychological Association, National Association of Social Workers, and Texas Chapter of the National Association of Social Workers (December 14, 1992).

5. *Anderson and Grubb* v. *Branen*, American Civil Liberties Union, Lesbian and Gay Rights Project, Docket 1993, p. 3.

6. *Colorado*, American Civil Liberties Union, Lesbian and Gay Rights Project, Docket 1993, p. 12.

Chapter 7

1. "Homosexuality," *Encyclopaedia Britannica, Micropaedia Edition* (Chicago: Encyclopaedia Britannica, Inc., 1993), p. 31.

Further Reading

Bodde, Tineke, ed. *Is Homosexuality A Sin?* Washington, D.C.: Federation of Parents and Friends of Lesbians and Gays, Inc., 1992.

Ellis, Lee. *Why Is My Child Gay?* Washington, D.C.: Federation of Parents and Friends of Lesbians and Gays, Inc., 1992.

Greenberg, David F. *The Construction of Homosexuality.* Chicago: University of Chicago Press, 1988.

"Homosexuality," *Encyclopaedia Britannica, Micropaedia Edition.* Chicago: Encyclopaedia Britannica, Inc., 1994.

"Homosexual Rights Movement," *Encyclopaedia Britannica, Micropaedia Edition.* Chicago: Encyclopaedia Britannica, Inc., 1994.

Ruse, Michael. *Homosexuality, A Philosophical Inquiry.* New York: Basil Blackwell, Ltd., 1988.

Shilts, Randy. *Conduct Unbecoming: Lesbians and Gays in the U.S. Military, Vietnam to the Persian Gulf.* New York: St. Martin's Press, 1993.

Whitlock, Katherine. *Bridges of Respect, Creating Support for Lesbian and Gay Youth.* Philadelphia: American Friends Service Committee, 1989.

Index